*To Tom McCarthy, whose idea it all was*

# Contents

# Note on the Translation

I owe a considerable debt of gratitude to Helena Drnovšek Zorko, former Ambassador of Slovenia to Ireland. I had decided to translate a woman poet when invited to take part in this series of books, partly because I had learned that, as with Ireland in the 80s, poetry in Slovenia was not what you might call actively receptive to women's voices, so there was a small opportunity to make a political point, and partly because I thought that the final texts might be more readily seen as versions of the author's originals if it was clear that the speaking voice was not mine as a man. The Ambassador made it her business to provide me with as wide a range of texts in translation as it was possible to obtain, and gave generously of her time in helping me find my way, at last, to the work I have chosen to translate.

I neither read nor speak Slovene. I am deeply indebted, therefore, to Ana Jelnikar who supplied me with meticulous line-by-line literal versions of these poems, and with minutely-detailed, illuminating scholarly notes – I was able to cross over into the territory of Barbara Korun's poems by means of a strong, well-engineered bridge. I am also deeply indebted to Barbara Korun herself for all those conversations in which we strove together to make my early, stumbling versions into poems as faithful as could be to the originals. Three minds, two dictionaries and a single purpose – I hope that between us we have managed to bring across into English something of the work of a quite singular and arresting poet.

There is a convention that the title of 'translator' is given in these circumstances to the person responsible for the final texts. I am happy to accept this title, provided it is understood to mean, inter alia, that I alone am to blame here for any ultimate failure there may be to convey the grace and power of language and thought in the original poems.

Theo Dorgan
Dublin 2005

# Part I

## Eurydice

When I come
I will not be singing,
I will simply be there.
I will be light
that makes flowers grow,
prompts people to make love.

Everything is possible. Everything.

Light pours from the belly.
All is forgiven,
all is settled.
Every leaf will be shivering with love.

# The Assumption

I lie on your shoulder.
Dusk like a great black poppy
nods in the valley.
The bright milk of the West
flows from the mountain peaks.
The warm earth is wide-awake,
steams in the evening grass.
Lower and ever closer, the sky's embrace.
Everything fading, dissolving into mist;
even your body is disappearing
into the deep, dark sky.

## White Room

A room, then, a white room,
walls bright with limewash,
white shutters, bare wooden floor;
a bed in this empty room
and, in the far corner, two rucksacks.
Through the wide-open window
the smell of pines breaking in.

Rasp of cicadas dying away.
A bed in this room, this white room,
a couple sprawled there in blank heat,
gazing into a sky so blue they
are drowning in distance.
Legs, hips, hearts are touching –
but their eyes are turned towards
the high blue, they are rapt in the infinite.
This is how souls touch,
how they go to each other
under the skin and deeper yet...

Do I cover you, all of you?
Do you find shelter, here in me?

Here in the quiet, souls in their silence
Pour one into another, bound
in filaments of light.
There are rainbow patterns
on the milky ceiling,
soft explosions of colour.

Is anything softer than your finger tips?
What do your lips taste of?
Let me taste your heart's pulse, let me

feel the blood sway in your veins.
I would lie here for hours
unmoving in the silence,
just listening.


The world breaks in the white blank of noon.
Everything falls away, only your closeness
is ever closer, ever more present and yes,
this is powerful, yes, I too am afraid;
I am being so careful
not to hurt you, not to hurt myself.

Slowly now, no need to hurry,
time falls away, space falls away,
now there is only you.
Like this, the sea opening before Moses.
Like this, the world opening before me.
All that there is beats in your body,
beats in your heart.
Let me be closer still, let me
be deeply, completely inside you. Let me be you…

And then, the miracle. With a word, a touch,
you admit me to the moonlit glade of your self.
I can wade through the undergrowth of your groin,
rest in the soft nest of your navel,
I can lick at your armpits as a deer licks her fawn,
I can flick at your little ears,
I can drill my tongue into the whorls of your heart.
Sweet shivering shakes my body, too,
I can taste your every perception, your every thought.
The membrane of solitude stretches and bursts,
I am flooded in waves of you.
I am entranced by your big toes,

your big toes bring me joy!
Coarse skin on your heels, imagine that!
What a wonderful playground, your body,
a surprise at every step. We are like children
at play in each other, at play in the infinite sea.
No fear yet. No shame yet.
Everything here is one: yourself, myself, the sea, the sea.

## Lioness

The lioness is my love for you, the tawny lioness
with her golden skin, her golden eyes.
She walks by my side always;
when I sit down to rest she lies beside me,
her face by my leg like a loyal dog.
I play with her, I lie down between her great paws
and let her toss me like her cub.
I feel the weight of her great paws,
the sharp precision of her claws.
I taste dead meat on her breath.

Now she is dying, the tawny lioness.
More and more she falters behind me,
hurrying to catch up with me when I rise.
I see the clotted blood that beads her snout.
She lies there on her side, she raises
her yellow, waning gaze to me.
I ask her: Where has your strength gone?
Where has your voice disappeared to?
I lay myself down between her weary paws,
I close my eyes with hers.

# Woman

O I am heavy with sorrows,
torn bare from the dream,
my skin bright with sweat,
my emptiness
throbbing and thirsting for you,
for your manhood.

Only step up to me,
close enough to touch,
and my thoughts and words
fly away —
I hunt for them, chase them and
give up.
Numb, all I can taste is you,
your man's closeness...
my hot skin says
reach for me, take me,
no more, O no more
promises dreams expectations
just take me,
so that my breast be not hard,
so that I no longer wake alone
to unborn children crying at midnight.

O let me lie down by a warm man's body,
the sharp smell of a man in my pillow,
my hot skin stretched tight
in a circle of bright light,
mouth tongue breath
pouring from you to me,
from me into you
from you into me
our bodies suffering a change

and pulsing, throbbing,
our bodies alien to us both
wanting to be one body and soul,
one soul shot through one body,
so that, fulfilled, you fly off
you soar into the sky...

I am between your hands,
I am in your mouth in this
breathing panting moaning,
in this rubbing of skin,
in flesh in blood in bones,
composed between my legs, compressed
under the sky, spilled
poured dispersed annulled
and everywhere everywhere present.

When I come to my senses
body in a body
body next to a body body body,
my loved one, my darling,
I am so infinite gentle that I move
so I don't hurt you, so that
your flowering now into blossom
be not disturbed,
your leaf-fall, your shattering,
your fall from heaven
your fall into me
my tired and melancholy man,
all into me

who am now grown strong and solid,
whole full earth
clear plant sap
dark animal blood,

shiny and solid human.
I can reach hundreds of miles
out into deep space
while you sleep
and I watch over you,
that nothing may hurt you.

Now in this night
I am everything, everything –
all of this earth, all of her people,
day and night,
war and love
and what falls between,
children and women and the old,
artists and politicians, everything
I am everywhere I am
in each new leaf that grows,
in the newborn child and foetus,
infinite, unrepeatable, unique.

## Stag

I wake to a warm stag's tongue between my legs,
the evening light comes horizontal in through open doors.
Gently he nuzzles my breasts, this stag, and licks me,
his coarse tongue warm on my vulva, my breasts, my face.
His scent intoxicates me – earth, moss, fear and decay –
the raw odour of instinct.
He lies down beside me against my smooth belly,
I run my hands over his matted hair.
He holds his head proud, he gazes away from me into the
                                                        woods.
His bare penis is reddening in the shadows of dusk.

Time thickens. I reach out into the dark, I touch a man's
                                                        body.
Desire flares in me, I am suddenly all heat.
He makes love to me simply, directly; he holds me close.
In his hands are the north wind and the south wind.
Rivers and oceans run through his body.
His mouth is warm and full of summer rain.
The room fills with songs of earth, of beyond our earth.
Sometimes a flash of moonlight reveals his face.

He does not look me in the eye, he protects me from
                                                        himself.
Sometimes when he is with me I no longer feel the ground.
Sometimes lust pools in his navel like a clear spring.
Sometimes he fountains, spewing lava.
He never hurts me.
With infinite care he turns me belly down on to the earth,
when he bites my neck and I smell his hot breath I know
I am to be spared.

With the coming of dawn I feel small horns in his hair.
Fur sprouts from his head to his back, his rump.
On his belly are sudden tufts of bestial grass.
He has a stag's head at daybreak, his eyes on me barely
                                                human.
Eyes from the other side of the frontier.
Absent-minded, his hands of horn caress me.
I watch his antlers burgeon and spread.

The scent of morning flushes the hut, he stands to go.
One brief glance at me as I stand in the door
and I am  split in two, I fall to the ground in flame.
I listen to the pock of sharp hooves going away,
I feel how my burnt halves are putting out flowers.

# Wolf

...and he is strange to me, strange, he who is all wolf and eats into my body from underneath, he shoves his snout into all my orifices and licks, licks, it is strange, so strange, I want to hide away, shrink into myself, escape into my head, be away, be off...I am afraid to feel this, afraid of my body, afraid to feel his body. He eats into me more, his mouth a maw, his teeth so sharp, devouring me, he is devouring me like a soft, juicy meal, tearing me open, pushing between my legs with his tongue, nose, jaw, pelt, paws, pestle...he rams it deep, in to the root, over and over and over again, into this body no longer mine, a pure violence I permit, I allow, I do not defend myself but I will not be washed away...I am soft and pliant, he tosses me like a rag doll, I think to myself that this is how it is, he is a man, I am a woman, this is how it should be, this is how it happens, he makes me thinner and thinner, only a thin membrane left, thin skin, thin...and then paradise flowers in my head, heaven in my body, heaven, no, not the heaven of the body...and still he is deep in me, shoving me, tearing me, pushing deep into me, searching, searching...but I am replete, full and fulfilled, bright and calm, so full to the brim that I do not care what it is with me now, I would not care if there was blood running, I am beyond all pain and pleasure and I know, I know that everything is going to be all right, I cannot trust this wolf but everything is going to be all right, the power that is in me now is stronger than he is, this power that is changing him, healing him, healing me, healing the wound...

# Mirror

A man leans over me
as over water.
He wishes to see his face
in my water mirror
but my water is dark,
dark and deep, will not
give back his reflection.
He searches, surprised
then amazed, and I am afraid
he will jump in, jump into me,
and find staring back at him
his own face there, dead.

## A Hymn to Dane Zajc

You carry the world inside your breast.
You feel the world grows out of you,
death grows out of you,
centre and source —
your own victim,
your own torment,
your own executioner,
your own love.
There is nothing that is not you.

You do not speak of this,
the light in the dark of your life.
You write out of pain,
and the joy comes from
your power to frame it.
How deep the abyss
when words fail you !

And then the morning comes,
resonant and clear,
silently painting the landscape
of your soul below.
Above you the pure sky-music,
the nectar of grace,
the bronze embrace.

# Language

*to Christian Bobin*

Language – river, pool under shade of spruce.
I lie on the bottom, on sand, the water
laving me. I look at it, I look through it
at sun and at shadow.
It cools me, it soothes and it saddens.
Language like water, to make cool.
The body, as Bobin says, made light,
the soul burned to transparency –
just so. This takes my breath away,
it's all too big, too much...
I nurse, I absorb, I knead sweetness
into the soul's body. He strokes my hair,
my face, my breasts, spills gently
across my hips like a spreading palm.
Language – words, rhythms, pulse of the heart.

# The Moon Will Cover Me

I have two animals,
A red one and a blue one.
When the blue one drinks,
the red one goes rushing about —
and vice versa.
I never can catch them, torn as I am
between the resting one and the rushing one.

I float a thought for bait,
far, far out over the plain.
They take no notice,
their snouts sniffing the infinite.

I will lay myself down in the long grass,
close to a well, and sink into sleep.
The moon will cover me.

They will come in the morning
with the first horizontal light,
tired, sweaty, foam on their muzzles.
Then we will go together to drink water.

## Sixth Poem

Oh so quietly, oh so infinitely quietly
it makes itself heard, this tiny keening hurt,
pecking at me by day,
flooding through me at night
when everyone is sleeping,
breaking me down slowly
into common dust.

# The Beginning

Everything there in silence —
Then, in a word, it all opens out.

# Part II

## Pythias

I sleep over the fissure;
sharp edges press against
my soul my heart my sex,
my warm breath pours
into the chasm,
a file of black ants.
O my thousand lives!

Now, now I breathe deep
the intoxicating breath
of all that is.

## The Touch

Late autumn:
from a gravid sky
words are sifting
to earth.

Osmosis, touch.

## Twilight

Again the stars
rotate the sky of evening;
the age-old patience
of the hills;
syncope of the heart,
a beat & it begins.

Deep in the petals
the shadows deepen
and stand clear.

# Soon

Soon you will be speechless and alone
*soon*
soon your skull
will be laved by grains of sand
*soon*
soon thirst
will blacken your tongue
*soon*
soon the desert wind
will pluck your white bones
*soon*

and your bowels,
all your soft innards
will be ripped out
picked apart
and left to dry
*soon*
soon you will be a grain among grains
soon you will sing
with the desert dunes
sifting
to nothingness
*soon*

then I will come to you
like the northern lights
in sky-colours
drawn to your desert song
your otherworldly voice
oh, I will come to you, I will come
*soon, soon*

34

# And Quite Forget

I should like to fall
into a rock crevice

the blink of an eyelash
a moment of hearing

the heart beat
when the world disappears

I should like to fall
into the abyss

## On a Black Summer's Night

I stepped out into the garden
to pluck a flower for you —

it shook its leaves in my face,
fought me stubbornly,
raked me with its thorns.

Now I wait for you
at the corner of the house,
I stand there

and feel
the rose trembling
in my hand,
its hot, black blood
leaking out
into the dark.

## *from* **Tangents**

### I

Flickers
of dry fear.
Sharp bites
of time.
Grey trembling
in the heart.
Delicate anxieties
in deep sleep.

### II

Husks from a tree
under the window
burst open;
black seeds
spill over branches in clumps;
empty, they whiten
in the twilight –

Home,
but foreign.

### III

I've missed it all,
everything's gone.
The day that might have been full,
things in quiet conversation.
I hold death close as

defeat or helplessness.
I wind back the thread — in vain.

A rustle of wings,
a kiss on the forehead.


## VI

We are:
dark gold of amber,
newborn light of leaf-bud
against lichen-grey wet sky.
Red tree branches are swollen eyelids,
some giant caught
in the melancholy moment.
New-woken creatures woven into the moss,
swift darting chirrups lance towards the sun,
the sun sinks to the bottom of the picture —
I dream, I am dreaming I touch you
with eyes wide open.


## VII

The summer glows,
reflected in waxed leaves.
All through the air,
the unloosed scent of honey.
Deep in the flowers
everything is busy,
even I am
bustling inwards.

X

The secret of longing:
song of the cicadas.
In sea salt is laid
the path to the beginning.

A conversation with you
is a prayer.
Light is
both dark and warm.

## Out of Evil Herb it Grows

You will get off at the last stop.
Clouds will be pointing to the south,
memory will be yellowing like paper.

In the net of the afternoon
a single glance will shatter
the glass in the eye of time.

There will be no blue in your footstep.
Along the coast a lattice of shadows
will muffle sound; your ears are stopped with pearls.

Odours of childhood in the creaking of crows,
dread in the scream of a white peacock
thawing inaudibly over the landscape.

Onto the shore of the future the tide
will wash skeletal bare trees;
your wounded arms, circled by swarming flies.

# The Notebook

First, you peel yourself.
You take a small peeling knife
and scrape off a layer of your self.
Sweet, salty fluids
come gushing out
through your pores.

Then, living bait,
you step out into the sun,
the salty sea,
the windy desert;
you wait for the words
to stick, to sting
and stay.

When you are covered in them
you step back in, poisoned;
you pick off
word after word,
you lay them out,
you arrange them in lines.

You're left there standing,
covered all over with small scars

## White Bulls

I open the window
and out of the night
white bulls leap into the room.
A dark figure
turns in her sleep.

Her skin is cold
Dutch linen,
light of the moon
in each crease and fold.
Her skin is silken
when it melts,
her underparts velvet
as she yields to me,
the forest moss of her sex.

A mouth accepts me,
a pool of rose water.
With my tongue
I draw damp lace
across her buds.

A blazing white landscape,
a lost traveller,
the rustling and crackling
blackness of her hair.

Tip of my tongue
on the taut skin of unhearing,
a string of gabbled syllables,
a high note plucked.

## Kiss

What word
sleeps on your lips,
what?

What landscape
glows beneath your eyelids,
what?

What voice
echoes
in the shell of the ear?

In the delicate fire of touch,
light rippling
from spread wings of gold.

## Flowers

Flowers —
valleys of flowers,
flowers in snow,
starry flowers,
ice-flowers
on windows,
flowers
in bed,
heavy-scented
flowers of your skin.

Roses in your mouth,
the prick and stab
of thorns.
I look for
traces of salt blood —
yours, mine —
in saliva;
I lick the heart-wounds —
mine, yours —
walled into a castle;
saliva, blood, milk.

My eyes wide open,
the breaking of dawn.

## My Heart Calls

My heart calls to you
quietly,
oh so quietly,
the pines embrace the wind
& the wind embraces time.
Time bumps against being,
soft as feathers.

I sit here under an arc
of light, trembling.
I trust
to the bone.

## The Turn

Moment by moment
a ripening, like blackberries
thickening
into sweetness

I find
I am weeping
at the golden reeds,
at the death of the sun.

## Cold Fire

Cold fire licks
my toes
shanks and knees,
cold fire
on a black rock,
cold fire
licking up my thighs,
up and up and in,
cold fire
will catch my hair,
my snake-dark eyes;
cold fire,
flaring fire,
oh cold fire
kisses hot —

I burn, burn, burn
in the pyre of myself.

## Towers of Karst

Noon embraced me
around the waist,
black traces of earth
on my white skin.

A red heart of flesh
pulsed, pulsed
beneath the horizon;
a small mouth
gulping, gulping
voraciously.

Out of the dark sun
a tear fell, smarting,
onto the white rock
into the rock cleft,
into two, into three.

A lizard flicked
into a crevice of the heart,
tickled the sky's aorta;
beneath a red-hot vulva
a key blazed,
a white flash.

In a magic circle
beneath the horizon of happiness
in a thicket of underground waters
in the twilight of desire
a child lay sleeping.

## Solace

I lie on my stomach
on the earth:

I draw up
damp and cold
for my bones,

dry heat
for my veins,

the calm & peace
of substance
for my thought.

## Breathing Together

You can
reach into me
anywhere
deep as you can;

in pleasure,
in pain
I slip away
from you;

in language,
in words,
here
you are breathing
me in,
you inhale me
completely.

# Part III

## Sisyphus

Through my dreams,
you roll a stone.
My body,
my heart,
groan in sleep.
You roll the stone,
your eyes
two slits of dark.
Above,
a surprise to me
over and over again,
you pounce on the stone
like an animal,
a body delighting
in movement;
when I catch up with you
you are already panting
in happy exertion.

Through my dreams
you roll a stone,
under my ribs the echo
of your terrible footfall.

# Birth

How pain like a fruit unpeels from inside its own skin, warm and gentle. How for the first time you feel the weight of the body. Now you are no longer flying, now you are here. Being here is your destiny, your first breath a scream as the earthly breaks into the delicate incarnate soul. This is why children's eyes are clear and glowing, why love joins what has never been separated. It only seems that the flash of the blade is what engendered yearning, began the measurement of time, because now there can be no passing away, not ever. In this tiny body everything is encompassed – a moment's flash and now it grows and it is.

Now light, clear light has colour and hardness and heat. It waits to be touched.

## I Saw a Man

I saw a man who carried death inside him, glowing, a bright flower, deep in his chest. He knew full well the weight of that fatal bloom, so beautiful in his breast, so very fragile. He carried that weight with infinite care, slowly (for time itself is powerless in that presence) staggering under the fullness of its weight. Out of respect, out of fear, we kept our silence. He sat there under the statue of the Mother of God, bathed in light flooding out of himself – death had opened the door in him. He couldn't see us, he couldn't see anyone, his feet planted on the void, his inward-turned eyes blind to broad daylight.

## Birth of an Angel

I gave birth out of a swelling on my breast, my third breast, long hidden under scarves and shawls. It hurt as it came. He helped me with his broad hands, he who husks out the shape of souls. I saw a small being, the size of a fist, covered all over with down, white and sticky. First you must let it dry, he said, warming the creature between his big fingers. I could see as it dried that this tiny being was wrapped in wings much bigger than itself. It didn't live, it couldn't, it didn't want to live. Apparition, sea-foam, it melted in our hands.

## Venice

I am in a coffin, sailing
into the city of water and death.
The black sky above me
is the eye of an evil bird.
I can move nothing
except my eyes. To left
and right of me the white glare
of palace and column.
Grace after death.

Then the bridge. And you –
Death has a face,
carved in soft stone.
Inaudible scream,
thrust though the seagull's
heart. What cannot be
recognized in dream.
Long echoes over water.

# My Mother

## I

My mother is sleeping, white in the whiteness, a white face with white wrinkles, white with softness. White time shreds into white flakes. The moment swells with whiteness. The voice falls, falls away into silence.

## II

My mother is sleeping, white bed in a white room. White patches of time nibble at her face. Whiteness. What should I do with my red heart in a white room? Blood, even before it falls, is absorbed in whiteness. Blood falls away, time falls away into the whiteness white.

## To Sleep in the Light

### I

To sleep in the light, at the very peak of light, on the summit, the summit of day, at noon. To fall asleep when strong currents of light are pouring through south-facing windows, to fall asleep in the hum of traffic, to fall asleep in the heart of town, between stone walls, to fall into sleep in the chewed core of the bed, alone.

To dream, to dream again it is the time of enveloping love, that time when lovers relish each other in the shell of light, tired, grown distant from so much love. "Why tears at noon, noon, when the day is at its height? I am coming, I will come again. Wait for me, hold me in dream, I am coming." Look, everything must pass: autumn turns into winter, the trees burst into bud, a downpour of light on sea, on sand, then Autumn again. Children grow up and leave us but love does not pass away. This love endures.

### II

Everything is yet to come, love, no reason to be afraid, the future you cannot see has not arrived yet. In the world of light, lotus-hearts are cracking open, in the centre of each a small, prematurely-born god. He needs to be fed, to be breast-fed with words, with acts, with – truth. Only truth counts where chaos pierces the hymen of the cosmos, floods into hot unrest. Here is beginning, here is birth, right at the tip of ending. Destruction, conception, building and ruin, everything is here and perfect. So, don't cry; the high sun pours down in vertical black rays and where it touches the earth small islands of beginning are springing up. Don't oversleep now, don't miss this sudden flourish of being, these thousands of eyes flashing with fatal beauty. I fear you will sleep and miss the beginning, forget to wake and be snuffed out for all eternity into this darkness at noon, where sadness and poems are all that remain to us.

## Every Breath You Take

And then the voice says: Shut down your reason, spread your wings and soar across the sky. Animals rise in the blood out of molten rock, a sea of burning floods me, I ride on an unknown animal, furred and warm. It licks my cheek. There is a tangle of strange creatures, fiddles played by melancholy donkeys, schools of transparent fish. Nostalgia. In this rock, in this wind, dolphins with flashing eyes, pulsing flocks of birds.

Wax of the human, sweet and salty and bitter, oozes from all pores, eyes are flooded with milk-acid of stars. Montes veneres, soft swelling olive trees, sweet buds of candied cherries.

Let me sink into you, grace of the gaze, scream of seagull, wind, warm wind that whips out of tiny stones, warm sway of an ass's back, fast cold olive trees, sea in its depths and in its colours washing over head and heart – an end to lamentation, an end to weeping: every breath you take now is a hymn.

# Note to the text

The poems in Part I are from *Ostrina Miline*, 1999.

The poems in Part II are from *Razpoke*, 2004

The poems in Part III are from *Zapiski Iz Podmizja*, 2003, with the exceptions of 'Sisyphus' which is from *Razpoke*, and 'Venice', which is from *Ostrina Miline*.

The poems in the collection *Razpoke*, though published in 2004, were for the most part written before those in *Zapiski Iz Podmizja*, hence our decision to select from *Razpoke* in Part II.